Plant-Based Diet Cookbook

365 Days of Cooking Healthy Greens to Lose Weight with Plant-Based Recipes Using 5-Ingredients or Less.

Aldrich Sinnayed

Table of Contents

INTRODUCTION

I was convinced that eating mostly plant-based foods that were not overly processed was the best thing for me.

Although my reasons for trying a plant-based diet were originally curiosity and then health-focused, I have also come to appreciate all the financial, ethical, and environmental reasons for enjoying this lifestyle.

Unprocessed plant-based foods are some of the cheapest foods around. In particular, root vegetables, rice, dried legumes, and beans are some of the most economical choices in the grocery store. For anyone living on a tight budget, switching to plant-based can be a financial game changer.

Whatever your reasons for choosing to eat more plants, this five-ingredient cookbook will help you start your journey.

Chapter 1: Plant-Based

Plant-Based Overview

Recently, "plant based" has become a buzzword in the food marketing world, seemingly showcasing plant-based products as wholesome alternatives to traditional animal-based foods. However, there can be a significant difference between a product labeled "plant based" and a whole food that's plant based. Just because an item on the grocery store shelf has a bright PLANT BASED logo on it does not necessarily mean it is a health-promoting food choice or a whole food.

Plant-based is a way of eating that revolves around whole or minimally processed vegetables, fruits, grains, mushrooms, legumes, berries, greens, spices, nuts, and seeds. Plant-based products are animal products, salt, oil, refined sugar, and highly processed plant-based foods. The goal is to eat food as close as possible to how it grows in nature. But don't think this means bland and repetitive. You may be surprised to find yourself eating a more diverse and flavorful diet as you learn about grains, spices, and vegetables that you may never have had on your plate before.

The Power of Plant-Based

Edible plants, such as mushrooms, potatoes, and watermelon, are packed with nutrients as nature intended, including phytochemicals, fiber, antioxidants, minerals, protein (amino acids), complex carbohydrates, and healthy fats. All these nutrients come together to perform a symphony within our bodies to maintain our health, including supporting brain function, repairing and growing tissue, maintaining muscle, eliminating waste, and regulating our bodily functions.

Eat mostly whole, unprocessed plants for optimal health. This means baked potatoes not potato chips, olives not olive oil, and strawberries not jam laden with refined sugar.

Studies have shown that plant-based foods can reverse coronary heart disease. type 2 diabetics have found that consuming plant-based foods repairs their insulin receptors, minimizing or eliminating their need for medication, rather than just controlling symptoms.

Less salt, oil, and sugar

Dishes omit added salt, oil, and refined sugar because of their negative health effects. Oil and refined sugar are both highly processed products that are devoid of the nutrients in the original plant, so just by definition, they are not whole or minimally processed. Most importantly, oil and refined sugar both have known health concerns associated with them.

Oil has been linked with the progression of type 2 diabetes and endothelium damage, which is a serious concern for the cardiovascular system. Oil and refined sugar both contribute to weight gain, and sugar has a significant negative impact on tooth decay and gut health. Salt can be consumed in excess and has been overused in our current food environment. Salt raises blood pressure and has negative impacts on artery function, which can be documented even 30 minutes after a single, salted meal.

How to Cook Without Oil

With a bit of practice and some simple tricks, you'll quickly excel at cooking without oil.

Oil Substitutes:

If a recipe calls for oil or oil-based products, such as margarine or mayonnaise, there are many substitutes you can use. Applesauce works well for baking, cashews can make dips thick and creamy, and avocado can add richness to condiments.

Omit Oil:

Amazingly, you can often simply omit the oil, and the recipe will still turn out great.

Use Water:

Vegetables can be sautéed without any oil. Mushrooms and onions contain enough moisture that you can fry them without oil. The key is starting with a hot pan and keeping a close watch to avoid sticking. You can add small amounts of water or vegetable stock to prevent the food from drying out.

Parchment Paper and Silicone Mats:

These will make a world of difference when cooking without added, processed fat. They prevent sticking but also make cleanup easier. I use parchment paper when cooking anything moist or sticky, such as recipes with fruit-based sauces or balsamic glaze, then simply toss the paper in the garbage. Silicone mats are useful for drier dishes and can be washed and reused. I mostly use them when baking or roasting, but parchment can also be cut to fit inside a frying pan to help prevent sticking.

Nonstick Cookware:

There are many types of nonstick cookware and bakeware available that are engineered to prevent food from sticking, which reduces or eliminates the need for oil. Some excellent options include ceramic, silicon-coated, and (my personal favorite) Heritage brand's The Rock collection.

Chapter 2: Snacks and Breakfast Recipes

Cashew Cream Zucchini Roll-Ups

Prep time: 10 minutes
Makes: 12 Roll-Ups

Ingredients:

- 4 tablespoons Cashew Cream, ranch version
- ⅓ cup matchstick or shredded carrots
- 1 bell pepper, thinly sliced
- ½ cup sprouted greens
- 1 medium zucchini

Directions:

1. With a vegetable peeler, cut the zucchini lengthwise into 12 ribbons.
2. Lay the ribbons out flat and spread 1 teaspoon of cashew cream at the end of each ribbon.
3. Top the cashew cream with the carrots, bell peppers, and sprouted greens.
4. Starting at the end with the toppings, roll up each ribbon and secure it with a toothpick.
5. Serve and enjoy.

Tip:

You can give these a southern flair by using different fillings, such as corn niblets, avocado slices, and a pinch of Chipotle Spice.

Per Serving: (3 roll-ups)

Calories: 70 | Fat: 4g | Protein: 3g | Carbohydrates: 8g
Fiber: 2g | Iron: 1mg

Queso and Sweet Peppers

Prep time: 5 minutes
Cook time: 5 minutes
Serves: 5

Ingredients:

- 3 tablespoons chopped fresh cilantro leaves
- 3 bell peppers, cut into sticks
- 1 cup Cheezy Sauce
- 1 jalapeño, diced
- 1 cup salsa

Directions:

1. In a nonstick pan, heat the cheezy sauce for 5 minutes over medium heat, until warm and smooth.
2. Transfer the sauce to a serving bowl and roughly mix in the salsa.
3. Top with the jalapeño and cilantro.
4. Immediately serve warm with the bell pepper sticks.

Tip:

Place the dip in a small electric slow cooker and keep warm.

Per Serving: (⅙ recipe)

Calories: 63 | Fat: 1g | Protein: 4g | Carbohydrates: 12g
Fiber: 3g | Iron: 1mg

Roasted Barbecue Nuts

Prep time: 5 minutes
Cook time: 15 minutes
Serves: 4

Ingredients:

- 2 tablespoons Chipotle Spice
- 2 tablespoons maple syrup
- 1 cup mixed raw nuts

Directions:

1. Preheat the oven to 300°F (about 148°C).
2. Line a baking sheet with parchment paper or a silicone mat.
3. In a bowl, combine the nuts and maple syrup. Mix to coat.
4. Add the chipotle spice and mix thoroughly.
5. Spread the coated nuts out on the lined baking sheet in a single layer.
6. Bake for 5 minutes. Stir and cook for 5 more minutes, then repeat for a total of 15 minutes of cooking.
7. The nuts continue roasting well after you remove them from the oven, so don't wait for any cue that they are done.
8. Allow to completely cool, then serve or store in an airtight container at room temperature for up to 3 weeks.

Tip:

Prevents bingeing on this high-fat whole food.

Per Serving: (1 ounce)

Calories: 207 | Fat: 16g | Protein: 6g | Carbohydrates: 14g
Fiber: 4g | Iron: 1mg

Breakfast Bean Burritos

Prep time: 10 minutes
Cook time: 5 minutes
Makes: 4 Burritos

Ingredients:

- 1 (9-ounce) can black beans rinsed and drained cooked
- 4 (10- to 12-inch) whole-grain tortillas
- 1 tablespoon Chipotle Spice
- ½ cup diced fresh tomato
- 1 cup Tofu Scramble

Directions:

1. Heat a nonstick pan over medium heat.
2. Put the beans and tofu scramble in the pan and heat until warm, about 5 minutes.
3. Lay the tortillas out flat and down the center of each, spread ½ cup of the bean-and-scramble mix.
4. Top with one-quarter of the tomatoes and a few pinches of chipotle spice.
5. Roll the burritos by orienting the filling horizontally, folding the bottom of the wrap over the filling, then folding in the sides and rolling up to close.
6. Serve immediately, or cool and refrigerate in an airtight container to consume the same day.

Tip:

If you have it on hand, you can use 1 cup of Mushroom Crumble in step 2 to fill out this burrito even more or as a substitute for the beans.
If you would like to freeze these, cut 4 pieces of aluminum foil. Tightly wrap the burritos individually, and place each burrito in a separate freezer bag. Reheat a burrito by removing it from the

freezer bag and foil and heating it in a microwave for 2 minutes, or in a 350°F (about 176°C) oven for 11 minutes until thoroughly warmed.

Per Serving: (1 burrito)

Calories: 312 | Fat: 7g | Protein: 14g | Carbohydrates: 50g
Fiber: 10g | Iron: 3 mg

Almond-Mango Muesli

Prep time: 5 minutes
Cook time: 15 minutes
Serves: 5

Ingredients:

- ⅓ cup unsweetened dried coconut (see tip)
- ½ cup dried mango, cut into ½-inch pieces
- 1 tablespoon ground cinnamon
- 1½ cups rolled oats
- ½ cup sliced almonds

Directions:

1. Preheat the oven to 350°F (about 176°C).
2. Line a baking sheet with parchment paper or a silicone mat.
3. In a medium bowl, combine the oats, almonds, coconut, and cinnamon.
4. Spread the mixture out evenly on the lined baking sheet. Sprinkle the mango on top.
5. Bake for 15 minutes or until the oats are browning and the mango is soft and sticky.
6. To serve warm, pour ½ cup of boiling water over ½ cup of muesli.
7. To serve cold, add ½ cup of muesli to ½ cup of unsweetened plant-based milk. If serving later, allow to completely cool and

refrigerate in an airtight container for up to 3 weeks.

Tip:

You can easily switch up this recipe's ingredients. Using the same measurements, try wheat bran, millet puffs, or whole rye instead of rolled oats.

Per Serving: (¼ recipe)

Calories: 295 | Fat: 14g | Protein: 8g | Carbohydrates: 36g
Fiber: 7g | Iron: 2mg

Mini Pizza Pockets

Prep time: 10 minutes
Cook time: 10 minutes
Serves: 5

Ingredients:

- 12 whole-grain mini pita pockets
- 4 tablespoons tomato paste
- 1 cup Cheezy Sauce
- 12 fresh basil leaves
- 1 cup mushrooms

Directions:

1. Dice the mushrooms into ¼-inch pieces.
2. In a nonstick pan, sauté the mushrooms over medium-high heat for 4 minutes until browned, adding water, 1 tablespoon at a time, as needed to prevent sticking.
3. Add the cheezy sauce and tomato paste. Heat for an additional 2 minutes over medium heat until warm.
4. Preheat the oven to high broil.
5. Cut openings into the pita pockets, along about two-thirds of their seam.

6. Fill the pita pockets with the warm cheezy sauce and mushroom mixture. Place each pita with the opening upward in the cups of a muffin tin. Depending on the size of your pitas, you may want one or two in each muffin cup.
7. Place 1 basil leaf in the opening of each pita.
8. Broil for 2 minutes, then serve immediately or refrigerate in an airtight container for up to 2 days.

Tip:

Don't overfill the pockets. Too much filling will make it difficult to eat.

Per Serving: (3 mini pitas)

Calories: 250 | Fat: 4g | Protein: 14g | Carbohydrates: 44g
Fiber: 9g | Iron: 5mg

Delicious Sesame Fire Crackers

Prep time: 10 minutes
Cook time: 10 minutes
Makes: About 70 Crackers

Ingredients:

- 1 tablespoon Shichimi Togarashi Spice Mix
- 2 tablespoons sesame seeds
- 4 tablespoons flax meal
- 1 cup whole-wheat flour
- ½ cup tahini

Directions:

1. Preheat the oven to 375°F (about 190°C).
2. In a small bowl, combine the flax meal with ½ cup of lukewarm water. Set aside for at least 4 minutes to congeal.
3. In a medium bowl, combine the flour and spice mix. Add the

tahini and flax mixture. Mix and knead by hand into a dough.

4. Set the dough between two large pieces of parchment paper, and use a rolling pin to roll the dough out to about ⅛-inch thick.
5. Remove the top piece of parchment and sprinkle the dough with the sesame seeds. Roll over the dough with the rolling pin to set the seeds into the dough.
6. With a sharp knife or pizza cutter, cut your desired cracker shapes. (Cut 1-inch squares or triangles)
7. Transfer the bottom parchment and crackers to a baking sheet.
8. Bake for 15 minutes, then set the oven to high broil and broil for 1 minute until the crackers are slightly browned.
9. Transfer the parchment and crackers to a cooling rack. Allow to completely cool. Store in an airtight container at room temperature for up to 1 week.

Tip:

I like to use a mix of roasted sesame seeds and black sesame seeds to top the crackers.

Per Serving: (5 crackers)

Calories: 100 | Fat: 6g | Protein: 3g | Carbohydrates: 9g
Fiber: 3g | Iron: 1mg

Spicy Guacamole

Prep time: 5 minutes
Serves: 2 to 4

Ingredients:

- 2 tablespoons freshly squeezed lemon juice
- 2 tablespoons chopped fresh cilantro
- 1 teaspoon Chipotle Spice
- ¼ cup diced sweet onion
- 3 Hass avocados

Directions:

1. Cut the avocados in half. Cross-cut the flesh in the skins, then scoop the flesh out onto a cutting board.
2. Add the lemon juice and mash together with a fork.
3. Place in a bowl or airtight container.
4. Mix in the cilantro, spice, and onion.
5. Serve immediately or refrigerate in an airtight container, with plastic wrap pressed against the surface of the guacamole to prevent air from reaching it, for up to 2 days.

Tip:

When avocado is exposed to air, it begins to turn brown. I try to make guacamole when I want it, rather than storing it before eating. If you need to store it or have leftovers, add a bit more lemon juice on top and press plastic wrap on top.

Per Serving: (¼ recipe)

Calories: 176 | Fat: 16g | Protein: 2g | Carbohydrates: 10g
Fiber: 7g | Iron: 1mg

Nutty Quinoa Granola

Prep time: 10 minutes Cook time: 25 minutes Serves: 4

Ingredients:

- 1 cup whole raw almonds
- 1 cup uncooked quinoa
- ½ cup peanut butter
- ¼ cup maple syrup
- 1 cup rolled oats

Directions:

1. Preheat the oven to 350°F (about 176°C).
2. Line a baking sheet with parchment paper or a silicone mat.
3. In a microwave-safe bowl, heat the peanut butter for 40 seconds, until melted.
4. Mix the maple syrup into the peanut butter. Add the oats, quinoa, and almonds.
5. Spread the mixture out on the lined baking sheet. Press down with a spoon to flatten the mixture.
6. Bake for 15 minutes until the granola starts to form solid sections.
7. Flip and stir slightly, then bake for an additional 10 minutes until turning brown.
8. Allow to completely cool on the baking sheet. Store in an airtight container at room temperature for up to 5 days or in the freezer for up to 2 weeks.

Tip:

This granola is delicious served on its own; with unsweetened plant-based milk, diced apples, or bananas; or as a topping on a plant-based yogurt.

Per Serving: (¾ cup)

Calories: 661 | Fat: 35g | Protein: 22g | Carbohydrates: 71g
Fiber: 12g | Iron: 4mg

Baked Spinach Dip

Prep time: 10 minutes
Cook time: 15 minutes
Serves: 5

Ingredients:

- 1 round loaf of pumpernickel or sourdough bread
- 2 tablespoons Savory Spice
- 2 cups fresh baby spinach
- 4 garlic cloves, minced
- 1 cup Cheezy Sauce

Directions:

1. Preheat the oven to 425°F (about 215°C).
2. Remove any large stem bases from the spinach. Chop the spinach coarsely.
3. In a nonstick pan, sauté the spinach and garlic over medium-high heat, adding tablespoons of water to prevent sticking, until the spinach wilts, about 4 minutes.
4. Add the cheezy sauce to the pan. Stir to combine and reduce the heat to low for 3 minutes.
5. Cut a large bowl shape into the bread loaf, creating a vessel for the dip. Retain the bread you cut out to serve with the dip later.
6. Pour the warmed cheezy sauce, spinach, and garlic into the bread bowl.
7. Sprinkle the top of the dip with the savory spice.
8. Place the loaf on a baking sheet. Bake for 15 minutes.
9. Remove and serve immediately while warm with the reserved bread.

Tip:

The art of creating sourdough bread is thousands of years old. It involves capturing wild yeast from the air and environment, rather than using commercially made yeast. Find a local bakery that makes wild yeast sourdough to reap the benefits of this traditional bread.

Per Serving: (⅙ recipe)

Calories: 262 | Fat: 3g | Protein: 11g | Carbohydrates: 51g
Fiber: 3g | Iron: 4mg

Tofu and Potato Hash

Prep time: 10 minutes
Cook time: 35 minutes
Serves: 4

Ingredients:

- 3 cups diced potatoes, cut into 1-inch cubes, rinsed
- 2 tablespoons Savory Spice
- 2 scallions, diced, for garnish
- 1 cup Tofu Scramble
- ½ cup salsa, for garnish

Directions:

1. In a microwave-safe bowl, steam the potatoes by filling the bowl with about 2 inches of water and then adding the potatoes.
2. Microwave, uncovered, for 8 minutes, stopping halfway through to stir. The potatoes will be slightly soft but not cooked. Drain the water from the potatoes.
3. Heat a large nonstick saucepan over medium-high heat.
4. Add the potatoes and savory spice. Mix to combine.
5. Cover and lower the heat to medium.
6. Cook for 20 minutes, until crispy, stirring occasionally.
7. Add the tofu scramble and cook for an additional 4 minutes, stirring occasionally, until hot.
8. Serve with the salsa and scallions, or allow to cool and

refrigerate in an airtight container for up to 3 days.

If you need a little help preventing sticking, you can line the pan with parchment paper.

Per Serving: (¼ recipe)

Calories: 146 | Fat: 2g | Protein: 8g | Carbohydrates: 26g
Fiber: 5g | Iron: 3mg

Dill Pickle Roasted Chickpeas

Prep time: 10 minutes, plus 1 hour to marinate
Cook time: 40 minutes
Serves: 4

Ingredients:

- 1 cup cooked chickpeas, rinsed and drained
- 1 teaspoon freshly ground black pepper
- 1 tablespoon garlic powder
- ½ cup apple cider vinegar
- 3 tablespoons dried dill

Directions:

1. Place the chickpeas and vinegar in a container and allow to marinate for 1 hour at room temperature.
2. Preheat the oven to 425°F (about 215°C).
3. Line a baking sheet with parchment paper or a silicone mat.
4. Drain the chickpeas. Lay out a clean tea towel or pieces of paper towel. Spread the chickpeas out on the towel. Pat them dry, removing any loose skins.
5. In a bowl, combine the chickpeas, garlic, dill, and pepper and mix.
6. Transfer the mixture to the lined baking sheet.

7. Cook for 40 minutes, stirring every 10 minutes, until the chickpeas are dried out and crunchy.
8. Allow to completely cool. Refrigerate in an airtight container for up to 7 days.

Can be used as a side dish for salads.

Per Serving: (¼ cup)

Calories: 74 | Fat: 1g | Protein: 4g | Carbohydrates: 12g
Fiber: 3g | Iron: 2mg

Arugula-Balsamic Flatbread

Prep time: 5 minutes
Cook time: 10 minutes
Serves: 4

Ingredients:

- 1 cup brown mushrooms, thinly sliced
- ¼ cup Maple-Balsamic Glaze, divided
- 2 whole-grain naan or similar flatbread
- 1 small sweet onion, thinly sliced
- ½ cup fresh arugula

Directions:

1. Line a baking sheet with parchment paper or a silicone mat.
2. In a nonstick pan over medium heat, combine the onion, mushrooms, and ⅛ cup of maple-balsamic glaze.
3. Cook for 5 minutes, until the onion caramelizes.
4. Turn the oven to a high broil setting.
5. Place the naan on the lined baking sheet, and top it with the onion-mushroom mixture.
6. Spread the arugula on top and drizzle with the remaining glaze.

7. Broil for 3 minutes, until the arugula starts to wilt. Keep a close watch to avoid burning.
8. Cut each flatbread into 4 pieces and serve warm.

Tip:

Instead of naan, there are a few popular WFPB bread brands. Your local grocery store may even make their own WFPB bread. Read through the ingredients and look for options with short ingredient lists, whole grains, and little to no salt, oil, or sugar. Watch for eggs and dairy as well.

Per Serving: (2 pieces)

Calories: 182 | Fat: 3g | Protein: 6g | Carbohydrates: 34g
Fiber: 3g | Iron: 2mg

Tomato and Dill Bagels

Prep time: 10 minutes
Makes: 4 Bagels

Ingredients:

- 4 tablespoons Cashew Cream, ranch version
- 4 whole-grain bagels
- 1 small Roma tomato
- 1 small red onion
- 2 dill sprigs

Directions:

1. Toast the bagels.
2. Thinly slice the tomato and onion.
3. Spread the cashew cream on the toasted bagels.
4. Top with the tomatoes, onion, and dill.
5. Serve and enjoy.

Tip:

Buy whole wheat bagels that happen to be plant-based and free of salt, oil, and sugar! Not all plant-based foods are marked as plant-based or vegan.

Per Serving: (1 bagel)

Calories: 310 | Fat: 5g | Protein: 13g | Carbohydrates: 58g
Fiber: 8g | Iron: 3mg
Balsamic Arugula Flatbread

Apple and Peanut Butter Snack

Prep time: 10 minutes
Serves: 5

Ingredients:

- 3 apples (about 2¾ inch in diameter)
- ¼ cup natural peanut butter
- ¼ cup dried cranberries
- ¼ cup pumpkin seeds
- ¼ cup rolled oats

Directions:

1. Slice each apple, with the core in the center of each slice. You should have 4 slices from each apple.
2. Cut the core out of each slice with a knife or round cookie cutter.
3. Spread each slice with 1 teaspoon of peanut butter, then top with 1 teaspoon of pumpkin seeds, 1 teaspoon of cranberries, and 1 teaspoon of oats.
4. Serve and enjoy.

Tip:

Keep a premixed airtight jar of pumpkin seeds, dried cranberries, and rolled oats so you can make this snack quickly.

Per Serving: (¼ recipe)

Calories: 259 | Fat: 12g | Protein: 7g | Carbohydrates: 35g
Fiber: 6g | Iron: 1mg

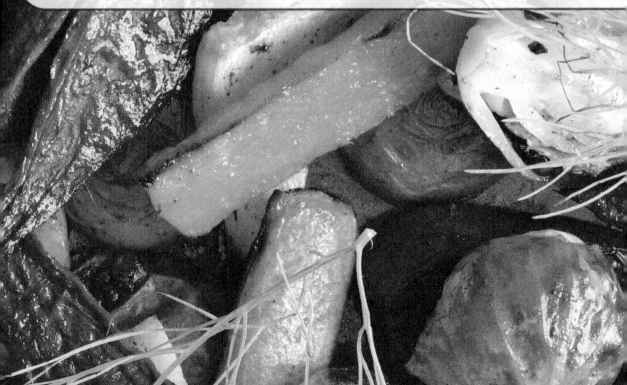

Chapter 3: Mains Recipes

Cheezy Broccoli Penne

Prep time: 5 minutes
Cook time: 55 minutes
Serves: 5

Ingredients:

- 2 cups broccoli florets, fresh or frozen
- 3 cups uncooked whole-grain penne
- ½ cup whole-grain bread crumbs
- 3 tablespoons nutritional yeast
- 2 cups Cheezy Sauce

Directions:

1. Preheat the oven to 425°F (about 215°C).
2. In a bowl, mix the cheezy sauce with ½ cup of water.
3. In a 9-by-13-inch casserole dish, combine the pasta and broccoli.
4. Pour the sauce over the top.
5. Sprinkle evenly with the bread crumbs and nutritional yeast.
6. Cover the dish with a lid or aluminum foil, and bake for 55 minutes, until the bread crumbs brown.
7. Allow to rest for 5 minutes then serve, or allow to cool and refrigerate in an airtight container for up to 3 days.

Tip:

Save all my whole-grain bread crusts in the freezer so that when I need bread crumbs, I can just grind them in the food processor to make my own.

Per Serving: (¼ casserole)

Calories: 435 | Fat: 5g | Protein: 23g | Carbohydrates: 81g
Fiber: 14g | Iron: 6mg

Sweet Cabbage Rolls

Prep time: 15 minutes
Cook time: 1 hour, 10 minutes
Makes: 17 Rolls

Ingredients:

- 1 medium green cabbage (about 5¾ inch in diameter)
- 2 cups Pineapple Barbecue Marinade
- 1 cup cooked whole-grain rice
- 2 cups Mushroom Crumble
- 3 garlic cloves, minced

Directions:

1. Preheat the oven to 400°F (about 204°C).
2. Line a 9-by-13-inch casserole dish with parchment paper or a silicone mat.
3. Cut the core out of the cabbage, down into the cabbage about 1 or 2 inches. This will make it easier to remove the leaves after cooking.
4. In a large stockpot over high heat, boil the cabbage with enough water to cover it for 20 minutes, just until the outside leaves are soft. Avoid overcooking; the leaves begin to fall off the cabbage in the water.
5. Meanwhile, make the filling by mixing the mushroom crumble, rice, and garlic in a bowl.
6. Drain the cabbage. Pull the individual leaves off. Remove any thick ribs from the leaves.
7. Lay out the leaves and spoon about 3 tablespoons of filling onto each. Fold the sides of each leaf over the filling and roll up. Use toothpicks to secure the rolls.
8. Lay them tightly together in the casserole dish. Cover with the marinade. Cover the dish with a lid or aluminum foil and bake for 40 minutes, until the sauce thickens.

9. Remove the cover and bake for an additional 10 minutes, until starting to brown. Serve hot or allow to cool and refrigerate in an airtight container for up to 5 days.

Tip:

If you don't have a large enough pot, you can also microwave a cabbage easily. Cut the core out as directed in step 3. Place it, cored-side down, in a microwave-safe bowl. Add ½ cup of water. Microwave for 10 minutes. Flip the cabbage and then microwave it for another 10 minutes.

Per Serving: (¼ recipe)

Calories: 301 | Fat: 2g | Protein: 9g | Carbohydrates: 70g
Fiber: 10g | Iron: 5mg

Taco Salad Rice Bowls

Prep time: 20 minutes
Cook time: 5 minutes
Serves: 4

Ingredients:

- 1⅓ cups Mushroom Crumble
- 1 cup cherry tomatoes, sliced
- 2 cups cooked brown rice
- 2 heads romaine lettuce
- 1 cup salsa

Directions:

1. In a nonstick pan, heat the mushroom crumble, rice, and salsa over medium heat and stir for 4 minutes until warm and fragrant.
2. Shred or chop the lettuce and divide it among 4 serving bowls.
3. Top each bowl with the heated taco filling and then garnish with the tomatoes.
4. Serve and enjoy.

Tip:

If you're preparing these ahead, store the lettuce, tomatoes, and filling separately in 3 airtight containers. You can then reheat the taco filling separately and build the bowls when you're ready to eat. If you want to elevate the presentation of these, you can find oil-free taco bowl baker sets. They will turn tortillas into crispy bowls in your oven or microwave.

Per Serving: (¼ recipe)

Calories: 219 | Fat: 2g | Protein: 10g | Carbohydrates: 45g
Fiber: 11g | Iron: 4mg

Delicious Curried Potatoes

Prep time: 10 minutes
Cook time: 20 minutes
Serves: 4

Ingredients:

- 3 cups diced yellow potatoes, cut into 1-inch cubes
- 2 tablespoons Garam Masala Spice Mix
- 1 medium yellow onion, diced
- 1½ cups vegetable stock
- 1 cup plant-based milk

Directions:

1. Combine the potatoes, onion, garam masala, plant-based milk, stock, and ½ cup of water in a deep nonstick saucepan with a lid.
2. Bring to a boil over high heat. Reduce the heat to medium-low and cover.
3. Simmer for 20 minutes, until the potatoes soften. Stir occasionally.
4. Serve warm or refrigerate in an airtight container for up to 5 days.

Tip:

Serve with whole-grain naan bread or brown rice.

Per Serving: (¼ recipe)

Calories: 114 | Fat: 1g | Protein: 3g | Carbohydrates: 24g
Fiber: 4g | Iron: 2mg

Jackfruit-Stuffed Sweet Potatoes

Prep time: 15 minutes
Cook time: 35 minutes
Makes: 12 Potato Halves

Ingredients:

- 6 small (4- to 6-inch) sweet potatoes, halved lengthwise
- 2 (16-ounce) cans of young green jackfruit, in water or brine
- 2 cups Pineapple Barbecue Marinade
- 1 small red onion or 2 shallots
- 4 cilantro sprigs

Directions:

1. Preheat the oven to 400°F (about 204°C).
2. Line a baking sheet with parchment paper or a silicone mat.
3. Place the potatoes, flat-side down, on the lined baking sheet. Bake for 25 minutes, until soft.
4. Meanwhile, drain and rinse the jackfruit. Cut the hard cores out of the jackfruit pieces.
5. Heat a nonstick pan over low heat. Pour in the marinade and jackfruit. Simmer until the potatoes are cooked.
6. When the potatoes are soft, remove them from the oven (leave the oven on). Spoon out about ¼ cup of cooked potato from each piece to make space to stuff them.
7. Fill each potato half with about ¼ cup of jackfruit, then return them to the oven for 8 minutes, until they are browning.
8. Meanwhile, dice the cilantro and onion. Remove the potatoes from the oven and top with the cilantro and onions.
9. Serve immediately or allow to cool and refrigerate in an airtight container for up to 2 days.

Tip:

Ensure you buy "young green," preferably in water and not ever in syrup, which is a sweet style not useful for this recipe.

Per Serving: (3 potato halves)

Calories: 373 | Fat: 1g | Protein: 5g | Carbohydrates: 89g
Fiber: 16g | Iron: 5mg

Sweet Onion Potatoes Scalloped

Prep time: 10 minutes
Cook time: 50 minutes
Serves: 4

Ingredients:

- 1 medium sweet onion, thinly sliced, rings separated
- 5 cups sliced yellow potatoes (¼-inch thick)
- 1½ cups unsweetened plant-based milk
- 3 tablespoons Savory Spice
- ¾ cup Cashew Cream

Directions:

1. Preheat the oven to 400°F (about 204°C).
2. Line a 9-by-13-inch casserole dish with parchment paper or a silicone mat.
3. In a medium bowl, mix the cashew cream, plant-based milk, and savory spice to make a sauce.
4. In the casserole dish, layer the potatoes and onion. Cover with the sauce.
5. Cover the casserole dish with a lid or aluminum foil and bake for 40 minutes, until the potatoes are soft.
6. Remove the cover and bake for an additional 10 minutes, until the top is beginning to brown.
7. Remove from the oven and serve immediately, or allow to cool and refrigerate in an airtight container for up to 3 days.

You can use any type of potato you have, but I find that yellow potatoes are sweeter and cook up softer than other varieties.

Per Serving: (¼ recipe)

Calories: 322 | Fat: 12g | Protein: 11g | Carbohydrates: 47g
Fiber: 6g | Iron: 4mg

Spaghetti Squash Boats

Prep time: 10 minutes
Cook time: 40 minutes
Serves: 4

Ingredients:

- 2 medium spaghetti squash
- 4 teaspoons Savory Spice
- ⅓ cup chopped fresh basil
- 5 garlic cloves, minced
- 1 cup Cashew Cream

Directions:

1. Preheat the oven to 400°F (about 204°C).
2. Line a baking sheet with parchment paper or a silicone mat.
3. Halve each spaghetti squash with a sharp knife, lengthwise. Spoon out and discard the seeds.
4. Lay the squash, cut side down, on the lined baking sheet. Bake for 40 minutes. Gently insert a knife into the bottom of one to make sure it's soft all the way through.
5. Meanwhile, heat a nonstick pan over medium-low and sauté the garlic for 4 minutes until it starts to brown. Add water, 1 teaspoon at a time, if the garlic is sticking.
6. Add the cashew cream, ½ cup of water, and the savory spice.

Mix to combine, remove from the heat, and cover.

7. Once the spaghetti squash is baked, remove it from the oven. Reheat the sauce over low heat while you prepare the squash.

8. On each of 4 small serving plates, place one squash half, cut-side up. Use a fork to loosen the stringy squash flesh.

9. Spoon the warmed sauce into the squash bowls, top with the basil, and serve immediately.

Tip:

Leave the spaghetti squash in their skin to serve, which doubles as a bowl, but you can alternatively remove all the stringy flesh from the squash and serve without the skins.

Per Serving: (¼ recipe)

Calories: 289 | Fat: 16g | Protein: 10g | Carbohydrates: 34g
Fiber: 6g | Iron: 4mg

Upside-Down Farmer's Pie

Prep time: 10 minutes
Cook time: 40 minutes
Serves: 4

Ingredients:

- 1 cup cooked corn kernels, canned or frozen
- 4 tablespoons Savory Spice, divided
- ½ cup whole-grain bread crumbs
- 4 cups diced yellow potatoes
- 1 cup Mushroom Crumble

Directions:

1. Preheat the oven to 400°F (about 204°C).
2. Line the bottom of a round 1½-quart casserole dish with parchment paper.

3. In a large pot over high heat, cover the potatoes with water and bring to a boil over high heat. Boil for 10 minutes or until soft.
4. Reserving ½ cup of the boiling water, drain the potatoes. In the pot, mash the potatoes with the reserved cooking water, adding 2 tablespoons of savory spice.
5. Transfer the mashed potatoes to the casserole dish. Press the potatoes down into a bowl shape, making about a 2-inch-deep bowl.
6. Put the corn in the bowl and sprinkle with 1 tablespoon of savory spice.
7. Mix the bread crumbs with the remaining 1 tablespoon of savory spice and top the potatoes with the mushroom crumble.
8. Cover and bake for 30 minutes, until the top begins to brown.
9. Serve hot or allow to cool and refrigerate in an airtight container for up to 5 days.

Tip:

I leave the skins on my potatoes when making this recipe to get all the vegetable's nutrients. Peeling the potatoes will result in a smoother potato texture.

Per Serving: (¼ pie)

Calories: 215 | Fat: 1g | Protein: 9g | Carbohydrates: 46g
Fiber: 7g | Iron: 3mg

Barbecue Romano Beans

Prep time: 5 minutes Cook time: 20 minutes Serves: 4

Ingredients:

- 2 cans Romano beans (3 cups cooked), rinsed and drained
- 2 cups Pineapple Barbecue Marinade
- 1 medium yellow onion, diced
- 1 teaspoon liquid smoke

Directions:

1. In a medium saucepan over high heat, sauté the onion for 3 minutes, until brown.
2. Add the beans, marinade, liquid smoke, and ¼ cup of water.
3. Reduce the heat to medium-low, cover, and simmer for 15 minutes, until the beans are soft and fragrant.
4. Serve warm or allow to cool and refrigerate in an airtight container for up to 5 days.

Tip:

When buying canned beans, look for low-sodium or no-salt-added varieties. You can cook beans from dry, which saves money but takes more time.

Per Serving: (¼ recipe)

Calories: 365 | Fat: 1g | Protein: 14g | Carbohydrates: 78g
Fiber: 14g | Iron: 7mg

Baked American-Style Goulash

Prep time: 10 minutes
Cook time: 40 minutes
Serves: 4

Ingredients:

- 1 (15-ounce) can of diced tomatoes, with their liquid
- 1 (13-ounce) box of whole-grain elbow macaroni
- 1 cup riced cauliflower, fresh or frozen
- 1 (15-ounce) can tomato sauce
- 4 tablespoons Savory Spice

Directions:

1. Preheat the oven to 400°F (about 204°C).
2. In a medium casserole dish, combine the macaroni, diced tomatoes, tomato sauce, cauliflower, and savory spice. Mix well.
3. Cover with a lid or aluminum foil and bake for 38 minutes, until the pasta softens.
4. Stir halfway through cooking.
5. Remove from the oven and serve warm, or refrigerate in an airtight container for up to 2 days.

Tip:

To make this dish heartier, substitute the riced cauliflower with my Mushroom Crumble.

Per Serving: (¼ recipe)

Calories: 411 | Fat: 3g | Protein: 18g | Carbohydrates: 84g
Fiber: 14g | Iron: 5mg

Carrots Quinoa Bowls

Prep time: 15 minutes Cook time: 20 minutes Serves: 4

Ingredients:

- 3 tablespoons Garam Masala Spice Mix
- 4 tablespoons Maple-Balsamic Glaze • 3 cups cooked quinoa
- 1 ripe Hass avocado   • 4 medium carrots

Directions:

1. Preheat the oven to 425°F (about 215°C).
2. Line a baking sheet with parchment paper or a silicone mat.
3. Cut the carrots in half lengthwise and then again across their middles, creating 4 pieces from each carrot.
4. Spread the carrots out on the lined baking sheet and bake for 20 minutes, until tender and browning. Remove from the oven when they are done.
5. In a medium bowl, combine the quinoa and spice. Mix well.
6. Cut the avocado in half and remove the seed. Use a spoon to scoop under the flesh and lift it out in one piece. Slice the avocado.
7. Build the bowls by placing ¾ cup of quinoa in the bottom of each of the four bowls, then 4 carrot slices, and then one-quarter of the avocado.
8. Drizzle with the glaze and serve immediately.

Tip:

If you have a group of picky eaters to feed, create a Buddha bowl bar. Provide a few cooked grains, cooked vegetables, spice mixes, and a few dressings to choose from. Everyone can build their bowl.

Per Serving: (1 bowl)

Calories: 301 | Fat: 9g | Protein: 8g | Carbohydrates: 49g
Fiber: 9g | Iron: 4mg

Fajita Rice Casserole

Prep time: 10 minutes
Cook time: 35 minutes
Serves: 4

Ingredients:

- 1 (15-ounce) can of diced tomatoes, with their liquid
- 3 tablespoons Chipotle Spice
- 3 cups cooked brown rice
- 1 red bell pepper, diced
- 1 green bell pepper, diced
- 1 cup Cheezy Sauce

Directions:

1. Preheat the oven to 400°F (about 204°C).
2. Line a 9-by-9-inch casserole dish with parchment paper. (The rice sticks, so it's easier to toss the paper than clean a silicone mat.)
3. In a medium bowl, combine the rice and chipotle spice.
4. Layer the ingredients in the casserole dish, with the rice on the bottom, topped with the tomatoes, then the cheezy sauce, and then the bell peppers.
5. Cover and bake for 35 minutes, until warmed through.
6. Serve warm or allow to cool and refrigerate in an airtight container for up to 2 days or freeze for up to 5 weeks.

Tip:

I allow it to cool well and store it in my freezer in 3-cup containers so I can quickly use it for recipes like this.

Per Serving: (¼ recipe)

Calories: 296 | Fat: 3g | Protein: 10g | Carbohydrates: 58g
Fiber: 8g | Iron: 4mg

Chapter 4: Basic Recipes

Shichimi Togarashi Spice Mix

Prep time: 10 minutes
Cook time: 10 minutes
Makes: 1 Cup

Ingredients:

- 2 tablespoons diced dried seaweed (nori)
- 5 tablespoons dried red chile peppers
- 6 tablespoons sesame seeds
- 3 tablespoons dried ginger
- 6 mandarin oranges

Directions:

1. Preheat the oven to 425°F (about 215°C).
2. Line a baking sheet with parchment paper or a silicone mat.
3. With a rasp or micro shredder, zest all 6 oranges' peels onto the lined baking sheet.
4. Bake the zest for 6 minutes, until dry, then remove from the oven and allow to completely cool for at least 1 hour.
5. Combine the zest, chile peppers, nori, and ginger in a spice grinder. Grind to a powder.
6. Combine the spice powder in the sesame seeds in an airtight container.
7. Store in a cool dry spot, such as a pantry, for up to 1 year.

Tip:

You can customize this blend by playing around with the ratios or by adding hemp seeds, garlic, or poppy seeds. Dehydrated orange peel is often sold in bulk stores. You can find dried seaweed (nori) as a snack or in larger sheets for making sushi.

Per Serving: (1 tablespoon)

Calories: 34 | Fat: 2g | Protein: 1g | Carbohydrates: 3g
Fiber: 1g | Iron: 1mg

Easiest Cashew Cream

Prep time: 5 minutes, plus 12 hours to soak
Makes: 1 Cup

Ingredients:

- 1 cup raw cashews

Directions:

1. In a container with a lid, cover the cashews with water, at least 1 inch above the cashews.
2. Set in the refrigerator for at least 12 hours to soak.
3. Once soaked, drain the water.
4. Put the nuts in a high-speed blender with 4 tablespoons of water.
5. Blend until creamy and smooth, about 90 seconds. To adjust the consistency, add more water, 1 tablespoon at a time, and blend until the desired consistency.

Tip:

Try adding these ingredients during blending in step 4, to create the different versions.

Mayo Version: 2 tablespoons lemon juice, 1 tablespoon apple cider vinegar, and 1 teaspoon black pepper

Ranch Version: 1 tablespoon onion powder, 1 tablespoon garlic powder, 1 tablespoon dried dill, and 1 tablespoon dried chives

Sweet Version: 5 tablespoons date paste, 1 teaspoon ground cinnamon, and 1 teaspoon vanilla extract

Per Serving: Ranch (1 tablespoon)

Calories: 49 | Fat: 4g | Protein: 2g | Carbohydrates: 3g
Fiber: <1g | Iron: 1mg

Per Serving: Mayo (1 tablespoon)

Calories: 46 | Fat: 4g | Protein: 2g | Carbohydrates: 3g

Fiber: <1g | Iron: 1mg

Per Serving: Sweet (1 tablespoon)

Calories: 53 | Fat: 4g | Protein: 2g | Carbohydrates: 4g
Fiber: <1g | Iron: 1mg

Cauliflower Mushroom Crumble

Prep time: 10 minutes Cook time: 10 minutes Makes: 3 Cups

Ingredients:

- 1 teaspoon freshly ground black pepper
- 3 cups fresh mushrooms, diced • 2 tablespoons liquid smoke
- ¼ cup diced cooked beets   • 1¾ cups diced cauliflower

Directions:

1. In a food processor or electric chopper, chop the mushrooms, beets, and cauliflower. Pulse 13 times until everything is finely diced but not a paste. Scrape down the sides of the bowl as you go to get an even chop.
2. Heat a nonstick pan over medium-high heat.
3. Combine the mushrooms, beets, cauliflower, and pepper in the pan, and dry sauté for 8 minutes, stirring regularly, until soft.
4. Add ¼ cup of water and the liquid smoke and continue sautéing for 2 minutes, until fragrant.
5. Allow to cool and store in an airtight container for up to 1 week.

Tip:

Don't have a food processor? Look for riced cauliflower and dice the mushrooms and cooked beets by hand.

Per Serving: (½ cup)

Calories: 20 | Fat: <1g | Protein: 2g | Carbohydrates: 4g
Fiber: 1g | Iron: <1mg

Peanut Sauce

Prep time: 5 minutes
Makes: 1 Cup

Ingredients:

- 1 teaspoon red pepper flakes
- ⅓ cup natural peanut butter
- 2 tablespoons maple syrup
- 2 tablespoons soy sauce
- 1 teaspoon garlic powder

Directions:

1. Combine the peanut butter, soy sauce, and ⅓ cup of boiling water in a bowl.
2. Stir to combine, then keep stirring for 3 minutes to get a smooth consistency. Add more boiling water, as desired, to thin it out.
3. Add the maple syrup, red pepper flakes, and garlic powder. Mix evenly throughout the sauce.
4. Allow to cool then refrigerate in an airtight container for up to 3 weeks.
5. Stir well before using because it may separate over time.

Tip:

If you have a peanut allergy, this sauce can also be made with ⅓ cup of raw almond butter in place of the peanut butter. The sauce will be slightly grittier because almond butter is not as smooth as peanut butter.

Per Serving: (2 tablespoons)

Calories: 78 | Fat: 5g | Protein: 3g | Carbohydrates: 6g
Fiber: 1g | Iron: <1mg

Savory Spice

Prep time: 5 minutes
Makes: 1 Cup

Ingredients:

- 1½ teaspoons freshly ground black pepper
- 7 tablespoons nutritional yeast
- 3 tablespoons dehydrated onion
- 4 tablespoons garlic powder
- 4 tablespoons dried basil

Directions:

1. Combine the nutritional yeast, basil, onion, garlic powder, and black pepper in an airtight jar.
2. Store in a cool dry spot, such as a pantry, for up to 1 year.

Tip:

Nutritional yeast comes in two types: one that is grown with added nutrients (fortified) and one without. If nutritional yeast is a new ingredient to you, the unfortified varieties tend to have a bolder cheesy, or nutty flavor.

Per Serving: (1 tablespoon)

Calories: 26 | Fat: <1g | Protein: 2.5g | Carbohydrates: 4g
Fiber: 1g | Iron: 1mg

Chipotle Spice

Prep time: 5 minutes
Makes: 1 Cup

Ingredients:

- 3 tablespoons dehydrated onions
- 5 tablespoons smoked paprika
- 2 tablespoons chipotle powder
- 3 tablespoons garlic powder
- 3 tablespoons ground cumin

Directions:

1. Combine the paprika, onions, garlic powder, cumin, and chipotle powder in an airtight jar.
2. Store in a cool dry spot, such as a pantry, for up to 1 year.

Tip:

If you don't have chipotle powder, you can use 2 tablespoons of chili powder instead. You can also substitute 2 tablespoons of onion powder for the dehydrated onions.

Per Serving: (1 tablespoon)

Calories: 22 | Fat: 1g | Protein: 1g | Carbohydrates: 4g
Fiber: 2g | Iron: 2mg

Pineapple Barbecue Marinade

Prep time: 5 minutes
Cook time: 10 minutes
Makes: 2 Cups

Ingredients:

- 1 cup crushed pineapple, with juices
- ½ cup unsweetened applesauce
- 3 tablespoons Chipotle Spice
- ¼ cup tomato paste
- ⅓ cup molasses

Directions:

1. Heat a nonstick pan over medium-high heat.
2. Sauté the tomato paste, stirring often, until it caramelizes and turns dark red, about 4 minutes.
3. Add the pineapple, molasses, applesauce, and chipotle spice.
4. Reduce the heat to low and simmer for 5 minutes, until fragrant, stirring occasionally to prevent sticking.
5. Allow to cool and refrigerate in an airtight container for up to 2 weeks.

Tip:

Canned crushed pineapple works perfectly for this recipe, but you can alternatively use fresh pineapple and achieve the same flavor. Chop it up and crush it in a blender or food processor.

Per Serving: (2 tablespoons)

Calories: 40 | Fat: <1g | Protein: 1g | Carbohydrates: 10g
Fiber: 1g | Iron: 1mg

Cheezy Sauce

Prep time: 10 minutes Cook time: 15 minutes Makes: 2 Cups

Ingredients:

- 2 tablespoons Cashew Cream or cashew butter (optional)
- 1 medium sweet potato, diced (2 cups)
- ⅓ cup unsweetened plant-based milk
- 1½ tablespoons Savory Spice
- ¼ cup nutritional yeast

Directions:

1. Put the sweet potato chunks in a medium saucepan and cover with water. Bring to a boil over high heat.
2. Reduce the heat to medium-high and cook for 15 minutes or until the potatoes are fork-soft.
3. Drain the potatoes and discard the skins.
4. Combine the potatoes, nutritional yeast, savory spice, plant-based milk, and cashew cream in a blender.
5. Blend for 2 minutes to a creamy smooth consistency.
6. Allow to cool and store in an airtight container for up to 1 week.

Tip:

Including cashew cream or cashew butter will make this sauce creamier, but it also adds calories and fat content. For anyone unable to consume nuts for any reason, you can simply omit it.

Per Serving: (¼ cup without cashews)

Calories: 51 | Fat: 1g | Protein: 4g | Carbohydrates: 8g
Fiber: 2g | Iron: 1mg

Per Serving: (¼ cup with cashews)

Calories: 39 | Fat: <1g | Protein: 3g | Carbohydrates: 7g
Fiber: 2g | Iron: 1mg

Maple-Balsamic Glaze

Prep time: 5 minutes
Makes: 1 Cup

Ingredients:

- 4 tablespoons yellow mustard
- ½ cup balsamic vinegar
- ½ cup maple syrup

Directions:

1. Combine the maple syrup, vinegar, and mustard in an airtight container.
2. Shake before using. Store in the refrigerator for up to 3 weeks.

Tip:

The price of balsamic vinegar varies widely, depending on its age, flavor, and thickness. If you want a thicker, more pungent balsamic, look for the more concentrated option.

Per Serving: (2 tablespoons)

Calories: 70 | Fat: <1g | Protein: <1g | Carbohydrates: 16g
Fiber: <1g | Iron: <1mg

Garam Masala Spice Mix

Prep time: 5 minutes
Makes: 1 Cup

Ingredients:

- 1 tablespoon dried cayenne pepper
- 2 tablespoons ground coriander
- 6 tablespoons curry powder
- 4 tablespoons garam masala
- 3 tablespoons ground cumin

Directions:

1. Combine the curry powder, garam masala, cumin, coriander, and cayenne in an airtight jar.
2. Store in a cool dry spot, such as a pantry, for up to 1 year.

Tip:

This recipe has a fairly mild heat. If you prefer no heat, simply omit the cayenne pepper.

Per Serving: (1 tablespoon)

Calories: 19 | Fat: 1g | Protein: 1g | Carbohydrates: 3g
Fiber: 2g | Iron: 2mg

Tofu Scramble

Prep time: 5 minutes
Cook time: 5 minutes
Makes: 3 Cups

Ingredients:

- ½ teaspoon freshly ground black pepper
- 1 (12-ounce) package firm tofu
- 1 teaspoon garlic powder
- ¼ cup nutritional yeast
- 2 tablespoons turmeric

Directions:

1. Heat a nonstick pan over medium heat.
2. Crumble the tofu by hand into the hot pan.
3. Add the nutritional yeast, turmeric, pepper, and garlic powder to the pan.
4. Cook for 4 minutes, until well combined and warm.
5. Allow to cool and store in an airtight container for up to 1 week.

Tip:

You can freeze this in an airtight container for up to 3 weeks.

Per Serving: (½ cup)

Calories: 85 | Fat: 3g | Protein: 9g | Carbohydrates: 6g
Fiber: 3g | Iron: 3mg

Lemon-Garlic Vinaigrette

Prep time: 5 minutes
Makes: 1 Cup

Ingredients:

- ¾ cup freshly squeezed lemon juice (from about 6 medium lemons)
- 1½ tablespoons freshly ground black pepper
- 4 tablespoons garlic powder
- ¼ cup apple cider vinegar

Directions:

1. Combine the lemon juice, vinegar, garlic powder, and black pepper in an airtight container.
2. Shake before using. Store in the refrigerator for up to 2 weeks.

Tip:

For a twist, you can make this with lime juice instead of lemon juice.

Per Serving: (2 tablespoons)

Calories: 26 | Fat: <1g | Protein: 1g | Carbohydrates: 6g
Fiber: 1g | Iron: 1mg

Chapter 5: Soups and Stews Recipes

Carrot-Tomato Bisque

Prep time: 10 minutes Cook time: 40 minutes Makes: 4 Cups

Ingredients:

- 1 (19-ounce) can of diced tomatoes, with their liquid
- ½ cup sun-dried or dehydrated tomatoes
- 1 cup unsweetened plant-based milk
- ½ cup sliced carrots (¼-inch coins)
- 2 tablespoons Savory Spice

Directions:

1. In a deep nonstick saucepan, bring 3 cups of water to a boil.
2. Add the carrots and boil for 10 minutes.
3. Add the sun-dried and canned tomatoes and the savory spice.
3. Reduce the heat to medium and cook, covered, for 30 minutes, stirring occasionally to prevent sticking.
4. Transfer the soup to a high-speed blender.
5. Add the plant-based milk and blend until smooth.
6. Serve warm or allow to cool and refrigerate in an airtight container for up to 6 days.

Tip:

You can make your dehydrated tomatoes. Preheat the oven to 275ºF (about 135°C). Line a baking sheet with parchment paper or a silicone mat. Slice tomatoes to about ⅓-inch thick. Sprinkle with freshly ground black pepper and put the tomatoes into the oven for 5 hours, until dried. You can store them in an airtight container in the freezer for up to 3 months.

Per Serving: (1 cup)

Calories: 91 | Fat: 1g | Protein: 4g | Carbohydrates: 17g
Fiber: 5g | Iron: 1mg

Edamame Miso Soup

Prep time: 10 minutes
Cook time: 10 minutes
Makes: 5 Cups

Ingredients:

- 3 tablespoons white or yellow miso paste
- ½ cup cooked edamame beans
- 1½ cups mushrooms, sliced
- 3 medium scallions, diced
- 2 cups vegetable stock

Directions:

1. In a medium pot, bring the stock and 3 cups of water to a boil.
2. Add the beans and mushrooms.
3. Reduce the heat to low and simmer for 10 minutes, until the mushrooms soften.
4. Remove the pot from the heat and add the scallions.
5. In a small bowl, mix the miso paste with ¼ cup of the warmed soup stock to dissolve, then stir the mixture into the soup. (The miso won't incorporate easily into the soup without first being thinned.)
6. Serve immediately or allow to cool and refrigerate in an airtight container for up to 2 days.

Tip:

Any tender vegetables or greens make a nice addition to this soup in step 2. The edamame beans I usually use in this recipe are frozen and already cooked. You can also top the soup with nori flakes.

Per Serving: (¼ recipe)

Calories: 67 | Fat: 1g | Protein: 6g | Carbohydrates: 10g
Fiber: 4g | Iron: 2mg

Spicy Peanut Ramen

Prep time: 5 minutes
Cook time: 10 minutes
Serves: 4

Ingredients:

- 1 tablespoon Shichimi Togarashi Spice Mix
- 4 servings of brown rice ramen noodles
- 1 cup cooked edamame beans
- ½ cup chopped scallions
- ½ cup Peanut Sauce

Directions:

1. Cook the noodles according to the package instructions.
2. Meanwhile, in a nonstick pan, combine the peanut sauce, beans, spice mix, and ½ cup of water.
3. Turn the heat to medium and simmer for 5 minutes, stirring occasionally, until warmed.
4. Drain the noodles and divide them among 4 bowls.
5. Top with the warmed peanut sauce and edamame.
6. Garnish with the scallions. Serve and enjoy.

Tip:

I love using frozen edamame for this dish. There's no need to precook it because it thaws fast in the sauce yet retains its firmness.

Per Serving: (¼ recipe)

Calories: 333 | Fat: 9g | Protein: 13g | Carbohydrates: 53g
Fiber: 5g | Iron: 2mg

Black Bean Chili

Prep time: 5 minutes
Cook time: 20 minutes
Makes: 5 Cups

Ingredients:

- 1 (15-ounce) can of diced tomatoes, with their liquid
- 1 (19-ounce) can black beans, rinsed and drained
- 3 tablespoons Chipotle Spice
- 2 cups Mushroom Crumble
- 1½ cups tomato sauce

Directions:

1. In a pot with a lid, combine the tomatoes, tomato sauce, mushroom crumble, black beans, and chipotle spice. Stir.
2. Bring to a boil over high heat and then reduce the heat to low.
3. Cover and simmer, stirring occasionally, until fragrant, about 20 minutes.
4. Serve warm or allow to cool and refrigerate in an airtight container for up to 6 days or freeze for up to 4 weeks.

Tip:

You can cook this soup in a slow cooker. Combine all the ingredients in the cooker, secure the lid, and cook on LOW for at least 2 hours.

Per Serving: (¼ recipe)

Calories: 199 | Fat: 1g | Protein: 13g | Carbohydrates: 37g
Fiber: 13g | Iron: 4mg

Tomatoes Lasagna Soup

Prep time: 10 minutes
Cook time: 15 minutes
Serves: 4

Ingredients:

- 1 (26-ounce) can of diced tomatoes, with their liquid
- 2 cups mini whole-grain lasagna noodles
- 2½ tablespoons Italian seasoning
- 2 cups Mushroom Crumble
- 1 tablespoon garlic powder

Directions:

1. Bring 5 cups of water to a boil and add the pasta noodles. Boil for 6 minutes.
2. Reduce the heat to medium and add the tomatoes, mushroom crumble, Italian seasoning, and garlic powder. Stir to combine.
3. Simmer for 5 minutes, until fragrant.
4. Remove from the heat and serve warm, or allow to cool and refrigerate in an airtight container for up to 3 days.

Tip:

Garnish with fresh basil or a dollop of Cashew Cream.

Per Serving: (¼ recipe)

Calories: 244 | Fat: 2g | Protein: 11g | Carbohydrates: 50g
Fiber: 10g | Iron: 3mg

Chilled Cucumber Soup

Prep time: 10 minutes, plus 30 minutes to chill
Makes: 4 Cups

Ingredients:

- 1 cup unsweetened plant-based milk
- 1 cup unsweetened applesauce
- 3 large English cucumbers
- 1 teaspoon garlic powder
- 1 red bell pepper, diced

Directions:

1. Peel, slice, and seed 2½ cucumbers. Set aside the unsliced cucumber half for later.
2. Combine the chopped cucumber, plant-based milk, applesauce, and garlic powder in a blender and blend for 60 seconds or until it reaches your desired consistency.
3. Chill the soup in the refrigerator for at least 30 minutes.
4. Slice the remaining half cucumber. Add the slices to the chilled soup.
5. Serve the soup cold, topped with the bell pepper.
6. Refrigerate in an airtight container for up to 3 days.

Tip:

You can use any kind of large cucumber for this recipe, but English cucumbers have fewer seeds and are ideal.

Per Serving: (¼ recipe)

Calories: 68 | Fat: 1g | Protein: 3g | Carbohydrates: 15g
Fiber: 4g | Iron: 1mg

Potato Harvest Stew

Prep time: 10 minutes Cook time: 15 minutes Makes: 5 Cups

Ingredients:

- 3 cups chopped, unpeeled yellow potatoes
- 1½ tablespoons poultry seasoning
- 1 small yellow onion, diced
- 3 tablespoons tomato paste
- 1 cup sliced carrots

Directions:

1. In a large stockpot, bring the potatoes and carrots to boil in 6 cups of water.
2. Boil for 8 minutes, until the potatoes are fork-soft.
3. Meanwhile, in a nonstick pan, sauté the onion.
4. Reserving 3 cups of the boiling water, drain the potatoes and carrots.
5. In the stockpot, combine the reserved cooking water, tomato paste, and poultry seasoning. Stir to combine.
6. Bring to a boil over high heat and then reduce the heat to low.
7. Add the potatoes, carrots, and onion. Remove from the heat.
8. Serve warm or allow to cool and refrigerate in an airtight container for up to 6 days or freeze for up to 4 weeks.

Tip:

Poultry seasoning is a common blend of herbs you can find at any grocery store. It is usually a mix of sage, rosemary, ground black pepper, and marjoram. It is perfect for stews, soups, and lentil loaves.

Per Serving: (¼ recipe)

Calories: 114 | Fat: <1g | Protein: 3g | Carbohydrates: 26g
Fiber: 4g | Iron: 2mg

Mushroom and Black Bean Stew

Prep time: 10 minutes
Cook time: 20 minutes
Makes: 5 Cups

Ingredients:

- 1 (19-ounce) can black beans (about 2 cups cooked), rinsed and drained
- 7 cups sliced mushrooms (about 1 pound)
- 3 tablespoons tomato paste
- 3 tablespoons Savory Spice
- 3 cups vegetable stock

Directions:

1. In a deep nonstick saucepan over medium-high heat, sauté the mushrooms for 10 minutes, until soft and brown. Stir often to avoid sticking. Add the stock, 1 tablespoon at a time, if needed to prevent sticking.
2. Add the beans to the pan, along with the tomato paste and savory spice. Stir to combine.
3. Bring to a boil over high heat, reduce the heat to low, cover, and simmer for 8 minutes. Stir occasionally.
4. Serve hot or allow to cool and refrigerate in an airtight container for up to 5 days.

Tip:

You can make this soup with a mix of cultivated and wild mushroom varieties. Some of my personal favorites are shiitake, cremini, portobello, trumpet, white button, and pink oyster.

Per Serving: (¼ recipe)

Calories: 181 | Fat: 1g | Protein: 14g | Carbohydrates: 32g
Fiber: 10g | Iron: 3mg

Bok Choy and Ginger Soup

Prep time: 10 minutes
Cook time: 20 minutes
Makes: 5 Cups

Ingredients:

- 4 tablespoons peeled and grated fresh ginger
- 3 medium carrots, cut into coins
- 2 tablespoons Savory Spice
- 2 cups vegetable stock
- 4 baby bok choy

Directions:

1. In a large stockpot, bring the stock, 3 cups of water, carrots, ginger, and savory spice to a boil.
2. Cover and reduce the heat to medium.
3. Cook for 15 minutes, stirring occasionally.
4. Chop the white bottoms off the bok choy, about 1 inch of the base. Cut the leaves lengthwise in half.
5. After the soup has cooked for 15 minutes, add the bok choy to the soup and bring to a boil once more.
6. Boil for 1 to 2 minutes until steamy hot.
7. Serve warm or allow to cool and refrigerate in an airtight container for up to 2 days.

Tip:

Don't peel those carrots! Nutrients are concentrated in the skins, so when possible, leave them on. Ensure the carrots are clean by scrubbing them with a vegetable brush under lukewarm water.

Per Serving: (¼ recipe)

Calories: 54 | Fat: <1g | Protein: 3g | Carbohydrates: 11g
Fiber: 3g | Iron: 1mg

French Onion Soup

Prep time: 10 minutes
Cook time: 50 minutes
Makes: 4 Cups

Ingredients:

- 4 medium onions, yellow or red, thinly sliced
- 3 tablespoons balsamic vinegar
- 1 tablespoon dried thyme
- 3 cups vegetable stock
- 3 dried bay leaves

Directions:

1. In a large nonstick saucepan, sauté the onions, stirring occasionally and adding 1 tablespoon of water at a time to prevent sticking, for about 25 minutes or until the onions are translucent and caramelized.
2. Add the vinegar and sauté for 5 more minutes, until the onions darken in color.
3. Add the stock, 2 cups of water, the thyme, and bay leaves.
4. Cover and simmer for 20 minutes, until thickened.
5. Remove from the heat and discard the bay leaves.
6. Serve hot or allow to cool and refrigerate in an airtight container for up to 2 days.

Tip:

For an authentic presentation, you can make bread tops for this soup. Use slices of a whole-grain baguette, top with a dollop of my Cheezy Sauce, and broil on high for 4 minutes.

Per Serving: (¼ recipe)

Calories: 68 | Fat: <1g | Protein: 1g | Carbohydrates: 15g
Fiber: 2g | Iron: 1mg

Noodle and Chick Soup

Prep time: 5 minutes
Cook time: 15 minutes
Makes: 5 Cups

Ingredients:

- 1 cup broken (1 inch) whole-grain linguine noodles
- 1½ cups mixed frozen vegetables
- 3 tablespoons Savory Spice
- ¾ cup cooked chickpeas
- 2 cups vegetable stock

Directions:

1. Combine the stock, savory spice, and 5 cups of water in a large pot.
2. Bring to a boil over high heat.
3. Once boiling, add the linguine noodles. Stir occasionally.
4. After 7 minutes of boiling, or once the noodles are al dente, reduce the heat to low.
5. Add the chickpeas and mixed vegetables.
6. Simmer for an additional 5 minutes or until the noodles are soft.
7. Serve warm or allow to cool and refrigerate in an airtight container for up to 2 days.

Tip:

Frozen vegetables are picked at their peak and flash-frozen to lock in their nutrients. I typically use a carrot, pea, and bean mix for this soup, but you can use any mix you like.

Per Serving: (¼ recipe)

Calories: 204 | Fat: 2g | Protein: 10g | Carbohydrates: 40g
Fiber: 7g | Iron: 2mg

Creamy Mushroom Soup

Prep time: 10 minutes
Cook time: 20 minutes
Makes: 4 Cups

Ingredients:

- 1½ cups unsweetened plant-based milk
- 5 cups sliced mushrooms
- 1½ cups vegetable stock
- 1 tablespoon dried thyme
- 5 garlic cloves, minced

Directions:

1. Heat a deep nonstick pan over medium-high heat and sauté the mushrooms and garlic for 10 minutes or until the mushrooms are soft. Add ¼ cup of water if the pan gets too dry.
2. Mix in the stock, plant-based milk, and thyme.
3. Reduce the heat to medium-low and simmer for 8 minutes, stirring occasionally, until the soup thickens.
4. Serve warm or allow to cool and refrigerate in an airtight container for up to 4 days.

Tip:

You can use mushroom stock to enhance the soup's flavor.

Per Serving: (¼ recipe)

Calories: 46 | Fat: 1g | Protein: 3g | Carbohydrates: 7g
Fiber: 1g | Iron: 2mg

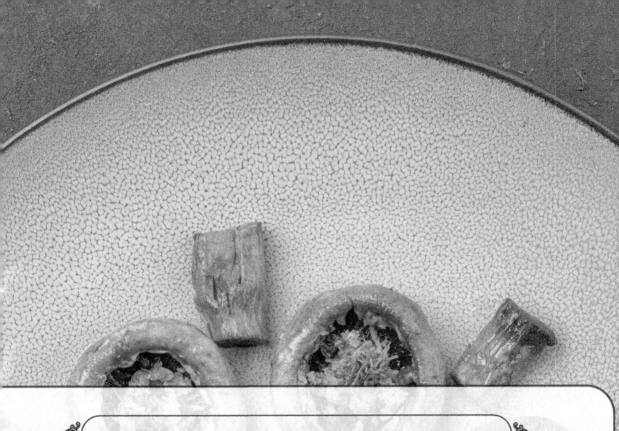

Chapter 6: Salads and Handhelds Recipes

Cabbage-Pistachio Salad

Prep time: 5 minutes
Serves: 4

Ingredients:

- 3 cups purple cabbage, thinly sliced
- ¼ cup raw shelled pistachios
- 2 tablespoons hemp hearts
- ¼ cup sunflower seeds
- ¼ cup balsamic vinegar

Directions:

1. In a large bowl, mix the cabbage and vinegar.
2. Serve immediately, topped with the pistachios, sunflower seeds, and hemp hearts, or refrigerate in an airtight container for up to 1 day.

Tip:

You can try Maple-Balsamic Glaze as an alternative dressing for this salad.

Per Serving: (¼ recipe)

Calories: 158 | Fat: 10g | Protein: 6g | Carbohydrates: 12g
Fiber: 3g | Iron: 2mg

Black Bean Quesadilla

Prep time: 10 minutes
Cook time: 10 minutes
Makes: 4 Quesadillas

Ingredients:

- 1 (15.5-ounce) can black beans, rinsed and drained
- 4 large whole-grain tortillas
- ½ cup Mushroom Crumble
- 1 tablespoon Chipotle Spice
- 1 cup Cheezy Sauce

Directions:

1. Heat a lidded nonstick pan over medium-high heat.
2. Place 1 tortilla in the pan to heat, flipping it every 15 seconds until it starts to bubble, about 45 seconds. Reduce the heat to low.
3. Top the tortilla with ¼ cup of cheezy sauce, ⅛ cup of mushroom crumble, and ¼ cup of beans.
4. Sprinkle with ¼ tablespoon of chipotle spice.
5. Cover the pan with a lid and allow to cook for 2 minutes.
6. Fold the tortilla in half and remove it from the pan.
7. Repeat for the remaining tortillas and fillings.
8. Slice each quesadilla into 4 triangles and serve warm, or allow to cool and refrigerate in an airtight container for up to 3 days.

Tip:

Serve these with salsa, guacamole, Cashew Cream, and fresh cilantro to garnish.

Per Serving: (1 quesadilla)

Calories: 367 | Fat: 7g | Protein: 16g | Carbohydrates: 63g
Fiber: 11g | Iron: 4mg

Apple-Potato Salad

Prep time: 10 minutes, plus 20 minutes to cool
Cook time: 10 minutes
Serves: 5

Ingredients:

- 3 cups diced yellow potatoes, cut into 1-inch cubes
- ¼ cup Cashew Cream, mayo option
- 1 tablespoon yellow mustard
- 1 cup Tofu Scramble
- 2 Fuji apples, diced

Directions:

1. Put the potatoes in a pot and cover them with water. Bring to a boil over high heat.
2. Reduce the heat to medium and cook for 8 minutes.
3. Drain the potatoes and allow them to cool.
4. Combine the cashew cream and mustard in a large serving bowl.
5. Add the tofu scramble and apples and mix.
6. Serve immediately or cover and refrigerate for up to 3 days.

Tip:

If you won't be eating this right away, I suggest dredging the diced apples in lemon juice before mixing them into the salad. This will keep them fresher longer and prevent browning.

Per Serving: (¼ recipe)

Calories: 233 | Fat: 6g | Protein: 8g | Carbohydrates: 39g
Fiber: 6g | Iron: 3mg

Summer Corn Salad

Prep time: 10 minutes
Serves: 4

Ingredients:

- ⅓ cup Lemon-Garlic Vinaigrette
- 1 head of butter or Boston lettuce
- ½ cup fresh blueberries
- 3 ears of cooked corn
- ¼ cup walnut pieces

Directions:

1. Roughly slice the corn kernels off the ears, leaving some larger chunks intact.
2. Pull the leaves off the head of lettuce.
3. Combine the corn, walnuts, vinaigrette, lettuce, and blueberries in a serving bowl. Toss to mix.
4. Serve immediately or cover and refrigerate for serving later the same day.

Tip:

Try grilling your corn after boiling it, to get a nice charred look.

Per Serving: (¼ recipe)

Calories: 154 | Fat: 6g | Protein: 5g | Carbohydrates: 25g
Fiber: 4g | Iron: 1mg

Lentil Sloppy Joes

Prep time: 5 minutes
Cook time: 15 minutes
Serves: 4

Ingredients:

- 1 can brown lentils (about 1¾ cups cooked), rinsed
- 4 tablespoons Chipotle Spice
- 1 red bell pepper, diced
- 1½ cups tomato sauce
- 4 hamburger buns

Directions:

1. In a nonstick pan over medium heat, sauté the bell pepper until soft, about 4 minutes.
2. Add the lentils, tomato sauce, and chipotle spice.
3. Reduce the heat to medium-low and cook for 10 minutes, stirring occasionally, until fragrant.
4. Serve warm on the buns, or allow to cool and refrigerate in an airtight container for up to 4 days.

Tip:

Serving these with yellow mustard, a pinch of black pepper, and hot sauce.

Per Serving: (1 sandwich)

Calories: 273 | Fat: 3g Protein 14g | Carbohydrates: 50g
Fiber: 9g | Iron: 7mg

Grilled Cheeze Sandwich

Prep time: 5 minutes
Cook time: 10 minutes
Serves: 4

Ingredients:

- 2 tablespoons Cashew Cream
- 8 slices plant-based bread
- ½ cup Cheezy Sauce

Directions:

1. In a bowl, combine the cheezy sauce and cashew cream. Stir to mix well.
2. Spread 2 ½ tablespoons of sauce onto each of the 4 slices of bread.
3. Top with the remaining 4 slices of bread to make 4 sandwiches.
4. Heat a nonstick pan over medium heat.
5. Lay the sandwiches in the pan and toast for 3 minutes, then flip and toast for another 3 minutes until brown and warm.
6. Serve and enjoy.

Tip:

These sandwiches go great with my Tomato-Carrot Bisque.

Per Serving: (1 sandwich)

Calories: 290 | Fat: 6g | Protein: 13g | Carbohydrates: 49g
Fiber: 11g | Iron: 4mg

Lettuce Wraps

Prep time: 10 minutes
Cook time: 15 minutes
Serves: 4

Ingredients:

- 1 head cauliflower, chopped into ½-inch pieces
- 2 bell peppers, thinly sliced
- 2 cups mung bean sprouts
- 2 heads romaine lettuce
- ½ cup Peanut Sauce

Directions:

1. Wash and separate the lettuce into single leaves so they are ready to be used as wraps or bowls.
2. Heat a nonstick pan over high heat.
3. Sauté the veggies in the following order, adding small amounts of water as you go to prevent sticking: Start with the cauliflower for 5 minutes. Leaving the cauliflower in the pan, add the bell peppers and cook for 4 more minutes, then top with the sprouts and cook for 4 minutes or until all the vegetables are soft.
4. Top the individual lettuce leaves with enough veggies to cover and drizzle with the peanut sauce.
5. Serve and enjoy.

Tip:

These work great for a buffet-style meal where everyone can build their wraps. You can make a beautiful spread of garnishes, such as chopped cilantro, sliced scallions, nuts, or seeds, so guests can customize their meal.

Per Serving: (¼ recipe)

Calories: 199 | Fat: 7g | Protein: 12g | Carbohydrates: 30g
Fiber: 13g | Iron: 5mg

Tofu Salad Sandwich

Prep time: 10 minutes
Makes: 4 Sandwiches

Ingredients:

- ¼ cup Cashew Cream, mayo version
- 1 small Roma tomato, sliced
- 1 cup Tofu Scramble
- 8 slices plant-based bread
- ¾ cup sprouts

Directions:

1. In a medium bowl, combine the tofu scramble and cashew cream.
2. Toast all the bread.
3. Spread the scramble mixture on 4 pieces of toast.
4. Top with the sprouts, tomato slices, and remaining bread slices.
5. Serve and enjoy. Unused tofu salad can be refrigerated in an airtight container for up to 3 days.

Tip:

You can also make this by substituting yellow mustard for the cashew cream in step 1.

Per Serving: (1 sandwich)

Calories: 335 | Fat: 9g | Protein: 16g | Carbohydrates: 51g
Fiber: 12g | Iron: 5mg

Hippie Sprout Salad

Prep time: 5 minutes
Serves: 2 As an Entrée, Or 4 As A Side

Ingredients:

- ½ cup cooked chickpeas (canned, rinsed, and drained, is fine)
- 1 cup cooked diced beets, cut into 1-inch cubes
- ⅓ cup Lemon-Garlic Vinaigrette
- ½ cup shelled raw pistachios
- 2 cups sprouts

Directions:

1. Combine the sprouts, chickpeas, pistachios, beets, and vinaigrette in a large serving dish.
2. Serve immediately or cover and refrigerate to serve later the same day.

Tip:

To grow your sprouts, all you need are some glass jars, like canning jars, with either some cheesecloth or wire-mesh lids, and some seeds. Sprouted seeds are available at most health food stores. The seed packs have specific directions, but all you have to do is rinse them with water a few times daily and leave them out on your counter for a few days.
That's it! It can't get any simpler to grow your food.

Per Serving: (1 entrée salad)

Calories: 300 | Fat: 16g | Protein: 13g | Carbohydrates: 33g
Fiber: 9g | Iron: 3mg

Lemon Pasta Salad

Prep time: 5 minutes
Cook time: 10 minutes, plus 20 minutes to cool
Serves: 5

Ingredients:

- 2 cups cooked and cooled whole-grain fusilli
- 2 cups cherry tomatoes, halved
- ¼ cup Lemon-Garlic Vinaigrette
- 1 cup minced fresh basil
- 1 cup shredded carrots

Directions:

1. Combine the pasta, basil, carrots, tomatoes, and vinaigrette in a serving bowl.
2. Serve immediately or cover and refrigerate for serving later on the same day.

Tip:

I love adding fresh garden peas to this salad.

Per Serving: (¼ recipe)

Calories: 146 | Fat: 1g | Protein: 6g | Carbohydrates: 34g
Fiber: 5g | Iron: 2mg

Winter Grapefruit Salad

Prep time: 5 minutes, plus up to 30 minutes to wilt
Serves: 2 As an Entrée, Or 4 As A Side

Ingredients:

- 1 medium grapefruit, cut into rounds
- ½ cup Maple-Balsamic Glaze
- 1 cup fresh cranberries
- 1½ cups sliced radish
- 3 cups kale

Directions:

1. Pull the leaves off the kale stems and then roughly tear the leaves into about 3-inch pieces.
2. Discard the stems and place the leaves in a large serving bowl.
3. Drizzle the glaze over the kale. Work the glaze onto the kale until the leaves are completely covered.
4. Set in the refrigerator to wilt for up to 30 minutes, to enhance the texture of the kale.
5. Add the radishes to the kale.
6. Toss to combine, then top with the cranberries and grapefruit.
7. Serve immediately or cover and refrigerate to serve later the same day.

Tip:

There are many varieties of kale out there, and some are tastier than others. Winter red kale and scarlet kale are my two picks for this salad. They're both grown in cooler temperatures, are available during the winter months, and are both salad-friendly varieties.

Per Serving: (1 entrée salad)

Calories: 249 | Fat: 1g | Protein: 4g | Carbohydrates: 58g
Fiber: 8g | Iron: 2mg

Smokey Carrot Dogs

Prep time: 10 minutes, plus 12 to 24 hours to marinate
Cook time: 35 minutes
Serves: 5

Ingredients:

- 3 tablespoons apple cider vinegar
- 6 medium (7- to 8-inch) carrots
- 1 cup Maple-Balsamic Glaze
- 2 tablespoons liquid smoke
- 6 hot dog buns

Directions:

1. Cut the carrots to the length of the buns.
2. Peel the carrots. (This is important because it allows the carrots to marinate properly.)
3. Bring a medium pot of water to a boil. Cook the carrots for 25 minutes, until fork-soft but not falling apart.
4. In a large airtight container or resealable plastic bag, lay the carrots in a single layer.
5. Top with the maple-balsamic glaze, liquid smoke, and vinegar. If the carrots are not completely covered, add just enough water to bring the marinade above the carrots.
6. Refrigerate for a minimum of 12 hours and up to 24 hours. The longer you marinate the carrots, the more flavorful they are.
7. When you're ready to cook, heat a nonstick pan over medium heat. Remove the carrots from the marinade and place them in the hot pan. Sauté the carrots for 7 to 10 minutes, using small amounts of the marinade to keep the pan wet, until browned.
8. Toast the buns and serve the carrots in them, topped with your favorite condiments.
9. Leftovers can be refrigerated in an airtight container for up to 2 days.

For an authentic barbecue look, you can give the carrot dogs grill marks with a chef's torch, or throw them on a hot grill after step 6.

Per Serving: (⅙ recipe)

Calories: 240 | Fat: 2g | Protein: 5g | Carbohydrates: 49g
Fiber: 3g | Iron: 2mg

Bean Sweet Potato Burgers

Prep time: 15 minutes
Cook time: 40 minutes
Makes: 5 Patties

Ingredients:

- 1 cup quick or rolled oats, plus more to adjust consistency
- 1⅓ cups diced unpeeled sweet potatoes
- 1½ cups cooked black beans
- ⅓ cup Chipotle Spice
- ¼ cup diced beets

Directions:

1. In a large pot, cover the sweet potato and beets with water and bring to a boil over high heat.
2. Cook until soft, about 18 minutes. Alternatively, you can microwave them in a microwave-safe bowl with about 1 cup of water for 9 minutes.
3. Preheat the oven to 425°F (about 215°C).
4. Line a baking sheet with parchment paper or a silicone mat. (I often sprinkle a few oats on the mats/paper as well, to help prevent sticking.)
5. In a large bowl and using a potato masher, or in a food processor, combine the sweet potato, beets, black beans, and

chipotle spice. Mash or pulse until almost smooth but leaving a bit of texture.

6. Place the mixture in a large bowl and add the oats. Combine by hand. The mix should be dry enough to form patties but still slightly sticky. If the mix is too sticky to form patties, add extra oats, 1 tablespoon at a time.

7. Using your hands, form the mixture into patties, about ¾-inch thick, to ensure even cooking.

8. Place the patties on the lined baking sheet. Bake for 15 minutes. Flip them and continue cooking for 7 more minutes, until firm.

9. Eat right away or refrigerate in an airtight container for up to 6 days.

Tip:

Allow these patties to cool fully and store them in freezer containers for up to 2 months.

If after baking and freezing you would like to be able to throw these on the grill, I suggest adding ⅓ cup of ground flaxseed in step 4.

Per Serving: (1 patty)

Calories: 281 | Fat: 3g | Protein: 11g | Carbohydrates: 56g
Fiber: 14g | Iron: 5mg

Chapter 7: Desserts and Smoothies Recipes

Banana-Blueberry Smoothie

Prep time: 5 minutes
Makes: 2 (12-ounce) Smoothies

Ingredients:

- 1 cup unsweetened plant-based milk
- 1 tablespoon hemp hearts
- 1 cup frozen blueberries
- 1 medium, ripe banana
- 1 tablespoon chia seeds

Directions:

1. Pour the plant-based milk into a high-speed blender, followed by the blueberries, banana, hemp hearts, and chia seeds.
2. Blend for 60 to 90 seconds, until smooth. Serve and enjoy.

Tip:

Hemp hearts are not always accessible, so you can substitute with 1 tablespoon of ground flaxseed, or simply omit the hemp hearts.

Per Serving: (12 ounces)

Calories: 193 | Fat: 6g | Protein: 4g | Carbohydrates: 32g
Fiber: 8g | Iron: 1mg

Mulled Apple Cider

Prep time: 10 minutes
Cook time: 1 hour
Serves: 6

Ingredients:

- 2 tablespoons whole cloves
- 10 sweet apples
- 2 cinnamon sticks
- 1 orange, sliced

Directions:

1. Peel, slice, and core the apples.
2. In a blender, blend the apples in three batches, using 1 cup of water for each batch, and blending until mostly smooth. There will likely still be some small pieces that don't blend, which is okay.
3. In a large stockpot over high heat, combine the apples, cinnamon, cloves, and orange.
4. Bring the mixture to a boil, then reduce the heat to low, cover the pot with a lid, and simmer for up to 1 hour.
5. When you're ready to serve, place a mesh strainer or doubled cheesecloth over a mug and ladle the cider through.
6. Enjoy immediately. Cool leftover cider, strain it, and refrigerate in an airtight container for up to 4 days. You can enjoy drinking this as a cold beverage, too.

Tip:

If you would like to have this simmer longer, maybe all afternoon while you host company, add a cup of water for every hour you would like it to simmer.

Per Serving: (⅙ recipe)

Calories: 144 | Fat: 0g | Protein: <1g | Carbohydrates: 39g
Fiber: 7g | Iron: 1mg

Chai Nice Cream

Prep time: 10 minutes, plus 1 hour 30 minutes to freeze
Serves: 4

Ingredients:

- ¼ cup unsweetened vanilla-flavored plant-based milk
- 4 ripe bananas, peel and chop into ½-inch pieces
- 2½ teaspoons ground cinnamon
- 1½ teaspoons ground ginger
- 1½ teaspoons allspice

Directions:

1. Line a baking sheet and a loaf pan with parchment paper.
2. Lay the pieces in a single layer on the lined baking sheet.
3. Place in the freezer to firm up for 1 hour.
4. Once frozen, put the bananas, cinnamon, ginger, allspice, and plant-based milk in a blender.
5. Blend for 90 seconds or until smooth. Add additional milk, 1 tablespoon at a time, if the consistency is too thick to blend.
6. Scoop the nice cream into the lined loaf pan and freeze for an additional 30 minutes, until it firms up.
5. Serve cold. Cover the loaf pan with a lid or plastic wrap to keep it airtight. Store in the freezer for up to 4 weeks.

Tip:

Use bananas that are spotted brown and overripe to get the softness and sweetness right for this recipe.

Per Serving: (¼ recipe)

Calories: 115 | Fat: 1g | Protein: 2g | Carbohydrates: 29g
Fiber: 4g | Iron: 1mg

Peanut Bliss Balls

Prep time: 10 minutes, plus 30 minutes to chill
Makes: 24 Balls

Ingredients:

- ¾ cup unsweetened shredded coconut, divided
- ½ cup unsweetened plant-based milk
- ½ cup natural peanut butter
- 1 cup pitted dates
- 1 cup rolled oats

Directions:

1. In a blender, combine the dates, peanut butter, and plant-based milk. Blend until smooth.
2. Transfer the mixture to a bowl and add the oats and ¼ cup of coconut. Mix well.
3. Chill the mixture in the freezer for 25 minutes, until the dough is firm.
4. On a flat surface such as a plate, spread the remaining ½ cup of coconut.
5. Using your hands, roll the chilled mixture into 1- to 2-inch balls, then roll them in the coconut.
6. Refrigerate in an airtight container for up to 7 days. They can be enjoyed straight from the refrigerator, but if you prefer, you can take them out 20 minutes before eating.

Tip:

You can substitute the coconut for cocoa for a peanut butter and chocolate version.

Per Serving: (2 balls)

Calories: 157 | Fat: 9g | Protein: 4g | Carbohydrates: 17g
Fiber: 3g | Iron: 1mg

Peanut Butter Cookies

Prep time: 10 minutes
Cook time: 10 minutes
Makes: 18 Cookies

Ingredients:

- 2 tablespoons ground flaxseed
- 1 teaspoon baking powder
- 1 cup natural peanut butter
- ½ cup pure maple syrup
- 1 cup whole-wheat flour

Directions:

1. Preheat the oven to 375°F (about 190°C).
2. Line a baking sheet with parchment paper or a silicone mat.
3. Combine the maple syrup and flaxseed with 1 tablespoon of hot water. Set aside.
4. In a medium mixing bowl, combine the flour and baking powder until crumbly.
5. Add the flaxseed mixture and combine by hand to form a dough.
6. Divide and roll the dough into 18 balls, each about 1½ inches in diameter.
7. Lay the balls out on the lined baking sheet. Use a fork to gently press the cookies down, just enough to indent them.
8. Bake for 7 minutes, just until they soften. Remove them from the oven and allow them to cool on the baking sheet for 5 minutes, then transfer to a cooling rack.
9. Enjoy warm or allow to fully cool and store in an airtight container at room temperature for up to 5 days.

Tip:

Storing natural nut butter is a bit different than storing processed nut butter that contains added oils, salt, and sugar. Take a container of natural nut butter and store it upside down at room temperature for at least 24 hours. After allowing it to sit, turn the jar right-side up, open it, and stir it well. Natural nut butter is separate into a thick nut paste and oil. This is not "added oil" but just the natural oils in the nuts.

Reincorporate the nut butter and then store it in the refrigerator. Keeping the nut butter cool will prevent it from separating again.

Per Serving: (2 cookies)

Calories: 267 | Fat: 15g | Protein: 9g | Carbohydrates: 28g
Fiber: 4g | Iron: 1mg

Raspberry Swirl Ice Pops

Prep time: 10 minutes, plus at least 6 hours to freeze
Makes: 8 Popsicles

Ingredients:

- ½ cup unsweetened plant-based milk
- 2 tablespoons vanilla extract
- 3 medium, ripe bananas
- ½ cup raspberries

Directions:

1. In a blender, blend the plant-based milk, bananas, and ½ cup of water until smooth, about 60 seconds.
2. Transfer 1½ cups of the mixture to a separate bowl. Mix the vanilla into the bowl.
3. Add the raspberries to the remaining mixture in the blender and blend until smooth.
4. Fill 8 ice pop molds, alternating between the banana-vanilla mixture and the raspberry one.
5. Freeze for 6 hours or until solid.

To add some color to the ice pops, place some unblended raspberries in the molds in step 4.

Calories: 55 | Fat: <1g | Protein: 1g | Carbohydrates: 12g
Fiber: 2g | Iron: <1mg

Savory Greens Drink

Prep time: 5 minutes
Makes: 2 (8-ounce) Smoothies

Ingredients:

- 1½ teaspoons freshly ground black pepper
- 8 fresh basil leaves or 1 tablespoon dried
- 1 cup peeled, sliced English cucumber
- 1 cup stemmed, chopped kale
- 1 cup baby spinach

Directions:

1. Combine the kale, cucumber, black pepper, spinach, and basil and 1 cup of water in a high-speed blender.
2. Blend for 80 seconds until smooth. Serve cold.

Tip:

You can turn this into more of a sweet green smoothie by adding a banana and substituting the water for unsweetened plant-based milk.

Per Serving: (8 ounces)

Calories: 18 | Fat: <1g | Protein: 1g | Carbohydrates: 4g
Fiber: 2g | Iron: 1mg

Melon Mini Cakes

Prep time: 20 minutes, plus 24 hours to chill
Serves: 7

Ingredients:

- 1 (13.5-ounce) can coconut milk (about 1¾ cups)
- ½ cup pure maple syrup
- 1 cup fresh blueberries
- 1 large watermelon
- 2 star fruit or kiwi

Directions:

1. Place the can of coconut milk in the refrigerator, upside down, for at least 24 hours before you want to make the cakes. Put the maple syrup in the refrigerator for at least 1 hour as well.
2. Chill a metal bowl and electric mixer whisk attachment in the freezer for 1 hour. Slice the watermelon in half and then into 2- to 3-inch-thick slices.
3. Open the can of coconut milk and discard the water. You should be left with a very thick coconut cream that is solid from being cold. Scoop the cream into the chilled mixing bowl and return the bowl to the refrigerator.
4. Wash the can, remove the label, and use it like a cookie cutter to cut out discs of watermelon. Set the watermelon discs aside.
5. Add the maple syrup to the coconut cream in the chilled mixing bowl. With an electric mixer fitted with the chilled whisk attachment, combine the coconut cream mixture until thick and smooth.
6. Spoon 1 tablespoon of whipped topping onto each melon disc. (You'll have leftover whipped topping, which can be refrigerated in an airtight container for up to 5 days.)
7. Top the whipped topping layer with a layer of blueberries.
8. Slice the star fruit, widthwise, to create star shapes. Using 3-inch

bamboo skewers to hold the stars in place, stand a single star on top of each melon cake. (You can also lay the star fruit flat on top of the cakes if you don't have skewers.)

9. Serve immediately or refrigerate for up to 3 hours before serving.

Tip:

There are lots of options for canned coconut milk, but only a few will work in this recipe. Make sure the only ingredients are coconut and water. If it has additives, such as guar gum, it will not work. It will need to be full-fat coconut milk as well, which contains about 15 grams of fat per ⅓ cup of milk. Nothing labeled "lite" or "low fat" will work.

Per Serving: (⅙ recipe)

Calories: 368 | Fat: 13g | Protein: 5g | Carbohydrates: 66g
Fiber: 4g | Iron: 2mg

Caramelized Bananas with Date Paste

Prep time: 20 minutes
Cook time: 10 minutes
Serves: 4

Ingredients:

- 1 cup fresh Medjool dates (about 8), pitted
- 1 teaspoon ground nutmeg
- 1 cup boiling water
- 2 ripe bananas

Directions:

1. In a glass measuring cup, measure out the pitted dates. Add the boiling water to the measuring cup until the dates are covered.

Set aside and let sit for 15 minutes.

2. Peel the bananas and halve them lengthwise, so the slices can lay flat.
3. In a high-speed blender, combine the softened dates and water.
4. Blend for about 60 seconds or until smooth.
5. In a nonstick frying pan, lay the bananas flat-side down. Don't be tempted to move them once they start cooking; leave them flat in the pan.
6. Turn the heat to high and cook for 5 minutes, until the bananas start to sizzle, then lower the heat to medium and spoon the date paste over the bananas.
7. Let simmer for 5 minutes, until the sauce thickens around the sides of the bananas.
8. Using two spatulas, move the banana slices to serving plates.
9. Sprinkle with the nutmeg and serve immediately.

Tip:

If you don't have a high-speed blender, you can purchase natural date paste.

Per Serving: (¼ recipe)

Calories: 188 | Fat: 1g | Protein: 2g | Carbohydrates: 50g
Fiber: 5g | Iron: 1mg

Cinnamon-Glazed Pears

Prep time: 10 minutes
Cook time: 15 minutes
Serves: 5

Ingredients:

- 1 (27-ounce) can pear halves (about 3¼ cups)
- 1 tablespoon ground cinnamon
- 2 tablespoons chopped pecans
- 2 tablespoons rolled oats
- ¼ cup pure maple syrup

Directions:

1. Preheat the oven to 400°F (about 204°C).
2. Line a baking sheet with parchment paper. (Don't use a silicone mat for this recipe; the syrup gets hard and can ruin the mat.)
3. Lay the pear halves, flat-side up, on the lined baking sheet.
4. Combine the maple syrup and cinnamon in a small bowl.
5. Sprinkle the pears with the oats and pecans.
6. Drizzle the maple and cinnamon glaze over all the pears.
7. Bake for 12 minutes, until warmed. Serve while warm.

Tip:

If you prefer to use fresh pears, cut four fresh pears in half, core them, and increase the cooking time to 40 minutes.

Per Serving: (¼ recipe)

Calories: 147 | Fat: 3g | Protein: 1g | Carbohydrates: 32g
Fiber: 5g | Iron: 1mg

Strawberry-Bean Smoothie

Prep time: 5 minutes
Makes: 2 (12-ounce) Smoothies

Ingredients:

- ¼ cup canned white kidney beans, rinsed and drained
- 1 cup unsweetened plant-based milk
- 1 teaspoon vanilla extract
- 2 cups frozen strawberries

Directions:

1. Pour the plant-based milk and vanilla into a high-speed blender, followed by the beans and strawberries.
2. Blend for 60 to 90 seconds, until smooth.
3. Serve and enjoy.

Tip:

This smoothie recipe doubles as an ice pop recipe.

Per Serving: (12 ounces)

Calories: 124 | Fat: 1g | Protein: 3g | Carbohydrates: 26g
Fiber: 7g | Iron: 2mg

Chocolate Pudding

Prep time: 10 minutes
Serves: 4

Ingredients:

- 3 ripe Hass avocados, cut in half and remove the seeds
- ½ cup unsweetened plant-based milk
- ¼ cup unsweetened cocoa powder
- 1½ tablespoons vanilla extract
- 3 tablespoons maple syrup (optional)

Directions:

1. With a spoon, remove the avocado flesh.
2. Combine avocados, plant-based milk, vanilla, cocoa, and maple syrup in a blender and blend until smooth, about 90 seconds. Adjust the consistency by adding more milk, 1 tablespoon at a time.

Tip:

If you want to consume the avocados immediately, find the darker ones and gently squeeze them to test their firmness. Look for one that feels more like a ripe banana than a hard apple. You can also pick off the small stalk at the end of an avocado. It should be a mild green color underneath, which indicates the avocado is not overly ripe.

Per Serving: (¼ recipe)

Calories: 203 | Fat: 17g | Protein: 3g | Carbohydrates: 13g
Fiber: 9g | Iron: 2mg

Tropical Pineapple Smoothie

Prep time: 5 minutes
Makes: 2 (12-ounce) Smoothies

Ingredients:

- 1 cup fresh or frozen pineapple chunks
- 1 cup coconut water
- 1 medium banana
- ½ cup frozen mango

Directions:

1. Pour the coconut water into a high-speed blender, followed by the pineapple, banana, and mango.
2. Blend for 60 to 90 seconds, until smooth.
3. Serve and enjoy.

Tip:

Make a batch of these smoothies and serve them at your next gathering as an alcohol-free drink. You can dress them up with slices of pineapple and cherries as garnish.

Per Serving: (12 ounces)

Calories: 140 | Fat: 1g | Protein: 2g | Carbohydrates: 34g
Fiber: 5g | Iron: 1mg

Maple-Blueberry Crisp

Prep time: 5 minutes
Cook time: 40 minutes
Serves: 5

Ingredients:

- 4 cups blueberries, fresh or frozen
- 2 tablespoons lemon juice
- ⅓ cup whole-wheat flour
- ½ cup pure maple syrup
- ¾ cup rolled oats

Directions:

1. Preheat the oven to 375°F (about 190°C).
2. In a medium baking dish, mix the blueberries and lemon juice.
3. In a separate bowl, combine the oats, flour, and maple syrup to make the topping.
4. Evenly spread the topping over the blueberries, then press down on the topping with your knuckles.
5. Bake, uncovered, for 40 minutes, until piping hot and brown.
6. Remove from the oven and allow to cool for 5 minutes before serving, or allow to cool and refrigerate in an airtight container for up to 2 days.

Tip:

Instead of using just blueberries, you can substitute a mix of blueberries, strawberries, and raspberries to make a mixed berry crisp.

Per Serving: (¼ recipe)

Calories: 280 | Fat: 2g | Protein: 4g | Carbohydrates: 66g
Fiber: 6g | Iron: 2mg

Cool Pumpkin Parfaits

Prep time: 10 minutes, plus 20 minutes to chill
Serves: 6

Ingredients:

- 2 cups pureed cooked pumpkin (canned or cooked from a fresh sugar pumpkin)
- 3 tablespoons pumpkin pie spice mix
- ¼ cup unsweetened plant-based milk
- ¾ cup Cashew Cream, sweet version
- ¼ cup pure maple syrup

Directions:

1. Combine the pumpkin, spice mix, and maple syrup in a small bowl. Mix well.
2. In another bowl, mix the plant-based milk and cashew cream with a hand mixer or whisk, until frothy.
3. In small serving vessels, make alternating layers with the spiced pumpkin mix and the cashew cream.
4. Place in the refrigerator to chill for at least 20 minutes before serving.
5. Serve cold within 1 day of preparing.

Tip:

Pumpkin pie spice mix is a premade blend of the perfect spices for pumpkin-based dishes and typically contains cinnamon, ginger, nutmeg, and cloves.

Per Serving: (⅙ recipe)

Calories: 170 | Fat: 8g | Protein: 4g | Carbohydrates: 24g
Fiber: 4g | Iron: 3mg

Mango Nice Cream

Prep time: 5 minutes, plus at least 40 minutes to freeze
Serves: 4

Ingredients:

- ⅓ cup unsweetened plant-based milk
- 1 cup frozen mango chunks
- 3 ripe bananas

Directions:

1. Line a baking sheet with parchment paper or a silicone mat.
2. Peel and slice the bananas into coins. Lay them out on the lined baking sheet.
3. Freeze the bananas on the baking sheet for at least 40 minutes.
4. Pour the plant-based milk into a high-speed blender, then add the bananas and mango.
5. Blend until smooth, about 90 seconds.
6. For a softer consistency, serve immediately. For a firmer consistency, put the nice cream into an airtight container and freeze for at least 30 minutes. Serve cold. Store in the freezer for up to 4 weeks.

Tip:

We like to make fresh, whole-food sundaes with this nice cream, such as slicing up a banana, adding a scoop of nice cream, and topping it with fresh cherries.

Per Serving: (¼ recipe)

Calories: 104 | Fat: 1g | Protein: 1g | Carbohydrates: 26g
Fiber: 3g | Iron: <1mg

Metric Conversions

1 teaspoon = 5 ml
¾ teaspoon = 3.7 mL
⅔ teaspoon = 3.3 mL
½ teaspoon = 2.5 mL
⅓ teaspoon = 1.6 mL
¼ teaspoon = 1.2 mL
⅛ teaspoon = 0.6 mL

1 tablespoon = 15mL
¾ tablespoon = 11 mL
⅔ tablespoon = 10 mL
½ tablespoon = 7.4 mL
⅓ tablespoon = 5 mL
¼ tablespoon = 3.7 mL
⅛ tablespoon = 1.8 mL

1 cup = 237 mL
¾ cup = 177 mL
⅔ cup = 158 mL
½ cup = 118 mL

⅓ cup = 79 mL
¼ cup = 59 mL
⅛ cup = 30 mL

1 ounce = 30 ml (Fluid)
½ ounce = 15 g
1 ounce = 30 g
2 ounces = 60 g
3 ounces = 85 g
4 ounces = 115 g
5 ounces = 142 g
6 ounces = 170 g

7 ounces = 198 g
8 ounces = 225 g
9 ounces = 255 g
10 ounces = 283 g
11 ounces = 312 g
12 ounces = 340 g
16 ounces = 455 g

4 pound = 1810 g
3½ pound = 1590 g
3 pound = 1360 g
2½ pound = 1130 g
2 pound = 907 g
1½ pound = 680 g
1¼ pound = 567 g
1 pound = 454 g
½ pound = 227 g

Printed in Great Britain
by Amazon

35114971R00064